THE GREAT I AM

THE GREAT I AM

American Titanic

Handri Timbuleng

Order this book online at www.trafford.com
or email orders@trafford.com

Most Trafford titles are also available at major online book retailers.

Printed in the United States of America.

ISBN: 978-1-4669-9729-5 (sc)
ISBN: 978-1-4669-9730-1 (e)

Trafford rev. 06/14/2013

 www.trafford.com

North America & international
toll-free: 1 888 232 4444 (USA & Canada)
phone: 250 383 6864 ♦ fax: 812 355 4082

CONTENTS

MAIL

How this happened   Tuesday, November 6, 2012 11:17 PM

"Barack Obama" <info@barackobama.com>

"HANDRI TIMBULENG" <timbuleng_handri@yahoo.com>

Handri --

I'm about to go speak to the crowd here in Chicago, but I wanted to thank you first.

I want you to know that this wasn't fate, and it wasn't an accident. You made this happen.

You organized yourselves block by block. You took ownership of this campaign five and ten dollars at a time. And when it wasn't easy, you pressed forward.

I will spend the rest of my presidency honoring your support, and doing what I can to finish what we started.

But I want you to take real pride, as I do, in how we got the chance in the first place.

Today is the clearest proof yet that, against the odds, ordinary Americans can overcome powerful interests.

There's a lot more work to do.

But for right now: Thank you.

Barack

Because you've saved your payment information, your donation will go through immediately:

QUICK DONATE: //   //   //   //   //

ACKNOWLEDGEMENTS

I have been encouraged in the writing of this book by "The Honor Letter" from the President of United State of America, is motivate me to move FORWARD with Educate the American citizen about their Future.

Special note: I writing this book to Malia and Sasha BO.

And I writing this book to my grandchildren: Victoria Quendelin Charles and Jason.

My hope and Prayer to you all, that God will be deliver from the perfect storm in the future.

And may God bless America and Israel.

PREFACE

Hi beloved reader, well come to my second book, and if you don't know my first book, The Image with sub title A Christian rethink Islamic terrorism and it is available in Barnes and noble book store or internet and in Amazon.com. The type of my book is mix between religion and the fact situation or it is like inspire from God and bring solution in the real world or some kind from spiritual realm to reality, and when I remember my first book need 3 years to get it done and cost a lot of money too, then when I get to my second book I feel like something impossible and don't have time, Imagine that I have to work from Monday to Saturday and it's start from 3 pm to 3 am or 72 hours a week, plus when i get home and just can fall in sleep on 4;00 am or 4;30,and then suddenly the alarm start ring 0n 5:30am and I have to prepare my wife lunch box, *make a hot tea and warm the car while my wife take a* bath and finally leaving to work on 6:00 am, so I am going back to sleep at 6:30am and suddenly on 10:00 am my granddaughter wake up and need me to make her milk, so I get up and make a milk in bottle and try to get back to sleep on 10:30am and then 12:00 am wake up and clean and prepare my lunch box and leaving the house on 2:30pm,and when I just arrived home on 3:30 am on Sunday(last work is Saturday and it's 3:00pm and went home on Sunday 3:00am),so I must prepare my bible reading to serve on my own church on 12:01pm-01:00pm,and just has burden on my soul, it is already a lot to say, like: how do I can get my church grow, cause already 3 years on the raw my starting baby step church, that is begin in the" house church" and step out moving to the real "church building" with sharing sanctuary of the United Church of Christ and then We must going back to the" house church" due to the growing of the church is not encourage me to stay in the church building, and I have to make me a decision to going back to the" house church". Working in two table is make me busy and suddenly has to add one more table, so it's three table at one time, seems like night mare for me in the first time, but I have to get this book done before it's too late, because we can't stop the time and we don't take it back the time that already past ! Chapter 1.1 So the story is star from: The Ponzi Scheme of Social Security. One of the earliest triggers of financial instability in America was the inception of Social Security. In 1935, during the presidency of Franklin Roosevelt, the Social Security Act was passed in to law. According to its architects, Social Security would rid our nation of all the evils associated with "old age "and make it possible for every American who lived to age sixty-five to have some kind of retirement income. Within four years of passing the Social Security Act, Congress amended the program to include survivor's insurance. In 1965 Medicare benefits were added. By 2008 Social Security and Medicare had swollen to a massive entitlement consuming more than $ 1 trillion-one-third of the federal budget. Today Social Security function as unfunded program. While it is true that government has raked in more in Social Security payroll taxes than it has paid out in benefits, that money is not protect in a trust fund, as many are led to believe.

The government uses the Social Security funds to pay for other program. There is no Social Security Trust fund. Social Security operates exactly like the scheme of Charles Ponzi. New contributors to the program fund the promises made to the older contributors. America workers who have faithfully paid their Social Security tax each year are relying on an empty federal purse to fulfill its promise to them. And today, according to most economists, we are about to enter the perfect storm. As New York Times economics reporter Edmund Andrews writes: The nation's oldest baby boomers are approaching 65,setting off what experts have warned for years will be a fiscal night mare for government." What a good country or a good squirrel should be doing is stashing away nuts for the winter "said William H.Gross, managing director of Pimco Group, the giant bond-management firm. "The United State is not only not saving nuts,it's eating the ones left over from the last winter. Social Security has become one of our ominous unsustainable programs leading to unending deficits. Richard Lamm, former governor of Colorado, summed it up like this: "Christmas is a time when kids tell Santa what they want and adults pay for it.Deficits are when adults tell government what they want and their kids pay for it" The next generation is paying for this generation's Social Security. How long before the system collapses under its own ever increasing weight?.

Before long I'd like to explain who is he? His name is Charles Ponzi born in March 03 1882 and pass away January18 1949 and the case is: The term Ponzi scheme is widely known description of any scam that pay early investor with ill-gotten funds from later investors. Ponzi scheme began shortly after the end of the First World War, Ponzi was charge with more with eighty counts of mail fraud. He spent three and half year in federal prison before he was deported and move to Rio de Jeniero, where he died in charity hospital in 1949. War and National Defense are one contribution to melt the American economic, and In 2008,41,5 percent of all the military expenditures in the entire world belonged to the United States. We spent more on National defense than China, Japan, Russia, Europe, and several other nations combine.

Economist Joseph Stieglitz, a Noble laureate, and his coauthor, Linda Bilmes, wrote a book about the cost of our current war, including its hidden costs. The book title, The Three Trillion Dollar War.

CHAPTER 1

The third Revelation from God. -The first Revelation is for America (is in my first book). -The second Revelation is for The President of United State (is in my first book). This time God give me the Third Revelation for America, And He start to speak the revelation to me to tell the America as a Government as a President, as Great Nation, "Help Israel" and I will taking care all the financial problem, or the Ponzi Scheme of Social Security.

This is the center of this book all about, and I just want to compare how much the price that God as The Great I am will bell out America, to Listen what He want, to be a" Defense of Israel". America will be collapse in 2030 as the economic debt at least 120.00 trillion US dollar and this is like a big ice mountain that get ready to destroy America as the Big Strong Ship like Titanic, and end up like the Titanic story because the ship hit the Big ice mountain. It's like the dark edge and blackness and tempest will waiting for our next generation, Understand that all the world wealth is 70.00trillion US dollar, what I am saying total of all bills in the world and all the bonds. All the world wealth is not cover American debt. So that how huge the mountain that will hit American ship in 17 years from now and is not that long to prepare the solution and to be ready for this perfect storm, and some people say that America is strong enough and impossible only one day America will Crass, Well Rome is not build in one day but only one day the Rome collapse with the same problem like we facing right know.(I used to visit Rome a view times and the place that I like the most is, Gladiator or the arena where a man will be fight with lion and people will make them as entertainment at that time or like we see soccer game or football game, and one of the amazing thing I will never forgot is, the map of how the Rome territorial in the whole world or Rome colony is 75 % of this world, Never in the history one nation can grab 75 % of this world country. But still what they say: Rome is not build in one day or overnight but only one day Rome must be collapse.

CHAPTER 2

5. Point of my concern is: 1. Regulation 2. Education. 3. Globalization. 4. Immigration. 5. Demoralization. I believe that in this time needed a Miracle, and for me miracle is: we do the necessary thing and God do the unnecessary,

1. REGULATION.

Regulation. Not every spending is bad and not every cut is good, I like President Bill Clinton give us his view on the challenges facing United State today and why government matters-presenting his ideas on restoring economic growth, job creation, financial responsibility resolving the mortgage crisis, and pursuing a strategy to get us "in the future business

"Clinton write," There is simply no evidence that we can succeed in the twenty first century with an antigovernment strategy "base on "a philosophy grounded in 'you're on your own' rather than 'we're all in this together'"He believe that conflict between government and the private sector has proved to be good politics but has produced bad policies", giving us a weak with not enough jobs, growing income inequality and poverty and a decline in our competitive position in the real world, cooperation works much better then conflict, and "Americans need victories in real life"

2. EDUCATION.

Education,in this challenging situation We don't need some education that teaching the student about how they need to be choose the job with security or 401 k and all the health insurance and indoctrination them with level of education make them earn more money and has the position in or the more title they has is more good position they can get, but we need to change their perspective from leaving under their mean to live with "Challenge is opportunity" And if you want to be success you must be "love complexity than simplicity" and motivate them to stand on their foot with doing their own business from a little, so they already start how to get money with taking care neighborhood dog and make some money or delivery newspapers, and challenge them about what will be happen in the future {there is no more middle class in America) so will be poor or rich, and explain them that only a little percentage of rich people in this nation so they has a big chance to be in this position, And they must like complexity to be a rich and must see the" challenge is not something that they must hidding from or has leave from it" but" challenge is opportunity", and give them example two difference job that make them work under one company and make them the owner of that company.

3. GLOBALIZATION.

Globalization.the climate and the raising of sea level and melting the ice, than the technology must be the big agenda to be concern in government agenda, and we need to learn the change of the culture and change of people behavior.

4. IMMIGRATION.

Immigration. Make sure that we don't let bad people enter this nation with their fake story of petition and the other hand has plane to destroy this nation(the example of BOSTON booming story) or let the border and all the airport the first gate to hold the problem to come.The other hand, so many good people live in this country and give a good contribution not get their paper work because of the lack of information and language barrier.

5. DEMORLIIZATION.

(A.)What is missing from this country ? and what is help America great ? The answer is "Honor and Respect"

Honor and Respect not only missing in America but in Church.

We are steady diet of disrespect to our programing to pop culture to our music through about everything around us, the market and advertising billboard, hate, distrust, disrespect toward authority.

When you get a little older what seem stupid when your younger Don't seem stupid anymore, My parent get officially smart, the time I got Married, up until that time parent are Idiot, Parent are betoken they don't know anything.

When you get a little older you find your mom and dad not dumb, you find out that the parameter that's good for you.

The reason Parent wrestle with your bonder of children life because parent care, if parent don't care you gone run loose and run wild.

The reason parent won't tolerate this

The reason parent got standing away

Because parent know the danger what you headed. The difference between parent and you is: you don't know what can happen and parent already know what can happen.

Parent is back from the future to tell you what can happen and hope you take parent wisdom instead of to relieve parent experience.

Everything in American situation has a key and one principle of the key is missing is honor.

WHAT EVER YOU HONOR IS DRAWN TOWARD YOU AND WHAT EVER YOU HONOR IS GIVES YOU ABILITY TO ACCESS.

WHAT EVER YOU DIRESPECT WILL MOVE AWAY FROM YOU AND WHAT EVER YOU DIRESPECT YOU WILL NEVER GET ABILTY TO ACCESS.

Difficult when we steady diet of disrespect

Man doesn't know how to respect women and Women doesn't know how to respect man.

People don't know how to respect government or leader.

If you Democrat or Republican is not the issue just honor as a senator or governor.

The fact is You can't honor that you don't agree with.

Whatever we like it or not" government is ordain by God "(Rome 13) so even if God got somebody in there you doesn't particulary like, their being used by that season to bring something that you don't see, another word: God has a big picture in Gods mind and you see in your little picture in your mind.

And God can lets thing fall apart for a little while just fill the government back up again.

You don't have any idea what God trying to do.

And the bible says if anybody in authority from Policemen to A President come in my presence is it immediately demand it to my honor and my respect.

I MAY DON'T LIKE THE WAY YOU LIVE YOUR LIFE,I MAY DON'T LIKE YOU BELIVE SYSTEM.

BUT THE POSITION THAT GOD HAS PUT YOU IN DEMAND THAT I RESPECT YOU IN THAT POSITION.

GOD CAN MAKE A THING HAPPEN TO YOU THAT IT'S WON'T HAPPEN TO SOMEBODY ELSE.

One real problem we got is: our media does nothing but disrespect, our news does nothing but disrespect, pop culture magazine do nothing but seatback and try to find dirt on one personal life of every celebrity.

Is amazing how quick they want to make them a celebrity till they can find the thing wrong with them and take them right down.

They love to make them raise fast but they love to watch them fall faster.

Heavy metal rock music have disrespect toward authority like crazy, disrespect toward parental authority, if your kids are drive in the head, it is hard to take the earphone from listening to that and turn around and honor their mother and mother.

Rap music disrespect toward woman and police and government.

(B) The Church.

Is the church has a contribution in demoralization? Answer is yes.

Why so many people prefer to get counseling to their problem with others than in they church? or they prefer to go to phisycologi than to the Pastor? even for their married problem that supposed to be the Pastor, but they are going to the other institution.

How the outsider see the church in their perspective? or the world people?

Church is the place that fill up with the people that know the rule, but they didn't do it

Church is fill up with the people that full of rule, but they didn't leave with the rule they full of.

The change of the teaching in church from to feed the follower to Bit or Gospel a good news to a bad news (always discourage not encourage).

In the front middle of the church always a stage is it call pulpit, and some church pull follower to the pit not take it out from the pit.

CHAPTER 3

Three more revelation from God to America:

1. From George III to George Washington to George george and Curious george.
2. America is checkmate.
3. confident with what you have.

1. From George III to George Washington to George George and Curious George.

In the past: The Declaration was the last American word In the argument between Great Britain and its American colonists. In 1763, the British Empire, the most successful and the freest the world had seen, had no more loyal subjects then colonists of the thirteen mainland colonies of British North American. Within two years, however, the first stirrings of disagreement between Britain and the colonists begun to disturb peace within the Empire.

In May 1776, the Second Continental Congress directed the colonies to frame new constitutions to replace their colonial chapters, Americans' commitment to liberty, the core principle of Anglo-American constitutionalism, was pushing them out of the Empire. That june. Richard Henry Lee of Virginia introduce three resolution in the Second Continental Congress, The first declaration that the colonies" are, and of right ought to be, free and independent states" On July 2, 1776, Congress adopted those resolution, two days later, it adopted a declaration drafted by Thomas Jefferson, setting forth the Americans 'case against George III and for independent.

From May 25 through May 28, The delegates elected their President, George Washington and their secretary, William Jackson of Georgia. And pass to George W Bush the father and the son (George George) And finally come to a kids movie Curious George. When this massage download to me I ask God why? and under my breath God speak to me, after George George whatever president elected going to be curious, how to lead this nation, or whatever president elected can't pay the national debt (now the national debt is 16,850,966 trillion / info by US Debt Clock.org) Sunday 5/12/2013 time 3:03 pm western time. And God says is not include the 2030 debt of 120.00 trillion WOW . . . AND God says this: it takes 204 year for America to have 1 trillion debt (from July 4 1776-November 4 1980) Ronald Reagan the president

THE DEBT CRISIS.

AND ONLY TAKE 20 YEARS AMERICA GET 14.3 TRILLION DEBT AND IT TAKES ONLY 1,5 YEARS TO GET 2,55 TRILLION MORE,OR IS USED TO 0.715 TRILLION PER YEAR, NOW RAISED TO 1,7 TRILLION PER YEAR, AND IF THIS HAPPEN CONTINUALLY THAN DEBT IN 5 YEARS GOING TO ADD 1.7 X 5 +16,850 = 25.3 trillion SO ABOUT 15 YEARS FROM NOW NATIONAL DEBT IS ABOUT 75,9 TRILLION OR ITS ABOUT 5 TRILLION OVER OF THE ALL THE WORLD WEALTH COMBINE (THE WORLD WEALTH ONLY 70 TRILLIO DOLLAR US/ALL THE BILL AND BOND IN THIS WORLD PUT IT TOGETHER) WOW, SO WHEN THIS HAPPPEN ? 2028 IS THE FIRST CRAZY STORM AND PLUS THE 2030 IS GOING THE PERFECT STORM OR 75,9 TRILLIO +3,4 TRILLIO +120 TRILLION PONZIE SCHAME AND TOTAL WILL BE 199.3 TRILLIO, OR IS ABOUT 3 TIMES THEN THE WORLD WEALTH . . . WOW

U.S.DEBT AND UNFUNDED OBLIGATIONS THROUGH THE INFINITE HORIZON.

One nation under God to One nation under Dog or its like the ship is tip over seems God tip over to Dog (TITANIC STORY)

2. AMERICA IS CHECKMATE.

The other down load is God gives me the image of chest board.

C H E C K M A T E.

Politics and Economic America is done.
Seems there is no way out.
Dead lock.
No more future.
Nobody can help.
The party is over.

God open the story about what happen in the past: 2 kings 6:25 And there was a great famine in Samaria: and behold, they besieged it, until an ass's head was sold for fourscore pieces of silver, and the fourth part of a cab of dove dung for five pieces of silver.

The worst is in first 26-29 Then, as the king of Israel was passing by on the wall, a woman cried out to him, saying." Help, my lord, O king!

And he said, "if the Lord does not help you, where can I find help for you? . . . then the king said to her, "what is troubling you? And she answered, "this woman said to me, 'give your son, that we may eat him today, and we will eat my son tomorrow 'So we boiled my son, and ate him. And I said to her on next day, 'Give your son, that we may eat him ';but she has hidden her son. WOW THAT A VERY SAD STORY EVER IN THIS WORLD.

In the past in Europe has the story of one bread cost one shopping cart full of bill/money, and when the mother leave the cart outside the store for a while and she find the pail of money still there but the cart is gone.

So in the other hand God want me to see what happen in His side as the fact is America is checkmate and all of this not come from God and He said: I will never make or act bad or for somebody be destroy by . . . (in the insurance cover always said if the bad happen is God act and is not been covered) and if good view they said Mother nature, In other word is God never do this for America but for sure is from devil or evil, and devil always said this: ha ha ha . . . America your now checkmate, But one voice from heaven said I DON'T THINK SO!

Its like believer has a bad report from the doctor and said you has cancer and you will leave only 3 month, but if we believe God the one who has the final word, not doctor report (the doctor just see what the reality), but believer must submit the final report to Gods hand and give it to Him. Don't let the devil has the final laugh and said you done, checkmate!

The same report of your house that the bank said, your house will be forclauser.

We must reject it in the name of Jesus Christ as THE GREAT I AM.

God introduce Him self as I am that I am what is mean I am here for you, I am the alfa and Omega, the author and the finisher, the beginning and the end,.

Psalm 46:1 King David said ".God is my strength and my refuge, Very presence help in trouble". (the situation king David when he has been chase by King Saul that want to kill him) and in the situation his sins with his chief commander Wife and sleep with her and end up kill her husband{likes adding sin to a sin)/he feels like all the foot in the world on his head and he feels that he reach the ground and no one can help him until he come to the God and asking for help for his lo life, and God come help and cover him from his mistake and forgive him, from his unjust weight.

Its like America now who has a lot of mistake in the past and like no one can help,REMEMBER THIS WHEN THE DOORS AROUND YOU HAS BEEN LOCK AND THE GROUND YOU STAND LIKE STEEL, ONE IS ALWAYS OPEN,AND ITS LOOK UP, YES LOOK UP,

3. CONFIDENT WITH WHAT YOU HAVE.

Yes look up, When Jesus has challenge to feet 15000 hungry people and find only has one boys lunch box and only has 2 piece of fish and 5 bread (it is a small bred and fish, because is belong to a young boys), And what He do is looks up and said thanks to God and the miracle happen.

What the lesson here is, we must learn not to complain one another and blame each other, but try to bring what we have and looks up, In the wilderness Moses has a problem to dead and has a limited time to get an action, and in the limited time God said: what you have ? and he said: only a rod, and God said to him to hit the water, and the water Departed, and all about a million people save from the enemy and even the ENEMY get kill too. WOW.

ONE real story about the girls has a heart to the kids and has a dream to give them a book to read in her community, so she is become a police women, and one day in her patrol she heard the alarm on in one big warehouse, and when she come in and turn the alarm off, she see the pile of book with note REJECT, AND SHE ASKING THE MANAGER IF SHE

CAN HAVE AL THAT BOOK, Finely she have 10.000 kids book in her hand to distribute to those kids in her community (she don't have that money and the connection) but her dream still came to pass.

And God just lead me to comeback in the story in 2 kings 7; 3-6, Now there were four leprous men at the entrance of the gate; and they said to one another, why are we sitting here until we die? If we say we will enter the city, the famine is in the city, and we shall die there. And if sit here we die also. Now therefor, come, let us surrender to the army of Syrian. If they keep us alive, we shall alive; and if they kill us, we shall only die". And when they rose at twilight to go to camp of Syrians; and when they had come to the outskirt of the Syrian camp, to their surprise no one was there. The lord had cause the army od the Syrians to hear the noise of chariots and the noise of a great army, so they said to one another "look, the king of Israel has hired against us the kings of the Hittites and the and the king of Egyptians to attack us!

Like America must have attitude ; we gone do something before we die, and God help to make the enemy run away. America need to change.

1. STUDENT YOU NEED CHANGE, YES YOU CANT,

2. BUSSINESS MAN YOU NEED TO CHANGE, YES YOU MUST

3. GOVERNMENT YOU NEED TO CHANGE, OR SOMEONE ELSE.

4. MILITARY YOU NEED TO CHANGE, OR MAKE IT ON FIRE. AND MAY GOD BLESS AMERICA, THE LAND OF HOPE AND THE LAND OF OPPORTUNITY, HOME FOR THE BRAVE.

IN JESUS NAME. HALELUJAH AMEN.

PREDICTION DEBT

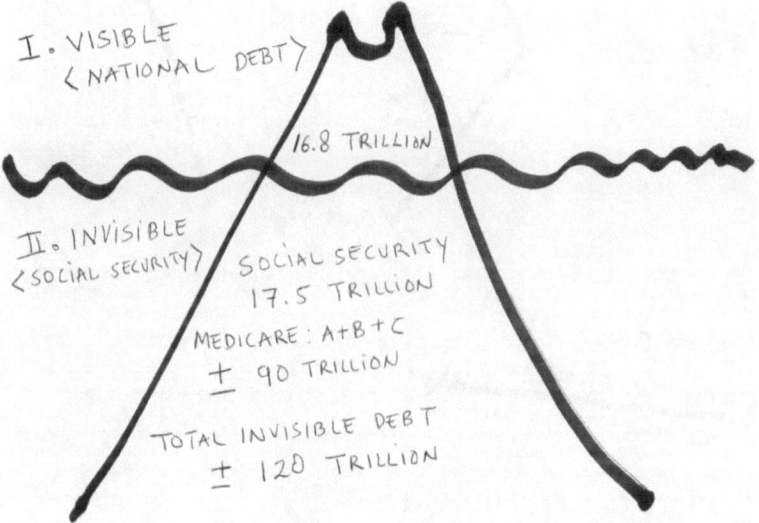

I. VISIBLE
⟨NATIONAL DEBT⟩

16.8 TRILLION

II. INVISIBLE
⟨SOCIAL SECURITY⟩

SOCIAL SECURITY
17.5 TRILLION

MEDICARE: A+B+C
± 90 TRILLION

TOTAL INVISIBLE DEBT
± 120 TRILLION

PREDICTION CLASS

AMERICA NOW

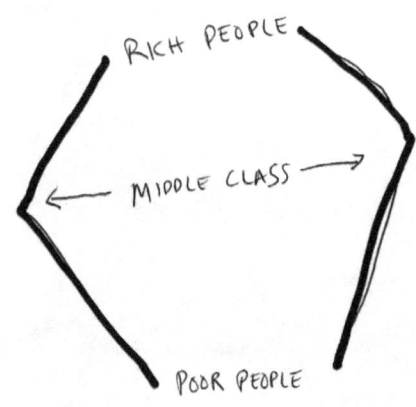

RICH PEOPLE

← MIDDLE CLASS →

POOR PEOPLE

MAY BE,
AMERICA AFTER CRISIS
⟨NO MORE, MIDDLE CLASS⟩

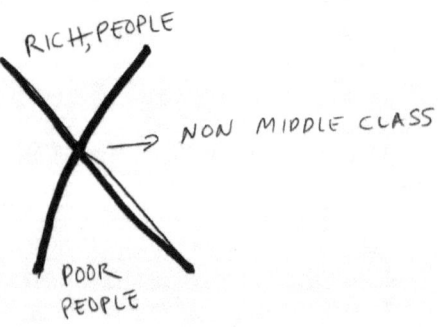

RICH, PEOPLE

→ NON MIDDLE CLASS

POOR
PEOPLE

Closing Word:

Deuteronomy 8:18

And you shall remember the LORD your God, for it is He (The Great I am) who gives you POWER to get WEALTH.

He is not only give America Wealth but P O W E R to get it.

Coming Soon NEXT BOOK TITLE:

1. American Threat
2. 100 Billion Dream
3. Christian Moslem and Heaven
4. Blood Money

Published Book:

The IMAGE: A Christian Rethink Islamic Terrorism

www.ingramcontent.com/pod-product-compliance
Lightning Source LLC
Chambersburg PA
CBHW061228280526
45784CB00006B/2678